Animal Prayers

Animal Prayers: 25 Poems

by

Randel McCraw Helms

© 2020 Randel McCraw Helms. All rights reserved.
This material may not be reproduced in any form, published,
reprinted, recorded, performed, broadcast,
rewritten or redistributed without
the explicit permission of Randel McCraw Helms.
All such actions are strictly prohibited by law.

Cover design by Shay Culligan

ISBN: 978-1-952326-77-6

Kelsay Books
502 South 1040 East, A-119
American Fork, Utah, 84003

For Susan
Eternal Delight

Acknowledgments

I wish to thank the editors of the following publications, both print and online, in whose pages seventeen of these poems first appeared:

An Elephant Never: "At a Wake of Elephants"

Blood & Bourbon: "Dog"

Civilized Beasts: "We Made the Seas Cloacal," "Last Things"

Dappled Things: "Gull," "The Breasts of Women and of Elephants," "*Dominus Illuminatio Mea*"

Emeritus Voices: "How Chukwu's Message Went Awry"

Good Works Review: "Koko Enters into Heaven"

The Orchards Poetry Journal: "Shepherd, Twenty-Four December," "The Wolf of Gubbio"

Red Wolf Journal: "In the Midst of Life We Are in Death"

Silkworm: "The Cat Who Stole My Heart"

Whale Road Review: "The Last Remaining Coastal Elephant"

Young Ravens Literary Review: "A Prayer for One Small Resurrection," "Recycle," "There Will Come Soft Rains"

Contents

A Prayer for One Small Resurrection	11
Koko Enters into Heaven	12
Gull	13
The Last Surviving Coastal Elephant	14
Last Things	15
We Made the Seas Cloacal	16
The Breasts of Women and of Elephants	17
A Tale of the Darasa of Eastern Africa	18
When My Mother Wept in Texas	19
In the Midst of Life We are in Death	20
The Cat Who Stole My Heart	21
Nothing Human Is Unique	22
Milton's Seeing-Eye Dog	23
Dog	25
The Wolf of Gubbio	26
A Shepherd, Twenty-Four December	27
When Elephants Dance	28
Dominus Illuminatio Mea	29
Life Builds Eyes at Need	30
At a Wake of Elephants	31
There Will Come Soft Rains	33
How Chukwu's Message Went Awry	34
Recycle	35
How the Fabled Toktokkie Beetle Prays for a Drink	36
A Prayer to Converse with Animals	37

A Prayer for One Small Resurrection

Once, just once, I assisted resurrection.
A friend presented me a fine bluefish,
Sea-wet and fat with recent feeding in the bay.
I took it to the shore to scale and clean.

Grimly slitting the distended belly,
I let fall a final meal, a mass of tiny fry,
All chewed and dead, save one. It squirmed alive
On the sand, yearning for its home, a yard away.

When does earth swerve for us, to yield such a chance?
I scooped a fist of grit and staring eyes
And flung it hard seaward, with a quick, small plea
That here, one time, was natural death defeated:

Let it unfurl, like silver leaves, to flash
And swim again toward life, to grow, and breed.

Koko Enters into Heaven

Koko, the lowland gorilla who learned American Sign Language, mastering more than a thousand expressions, died in her sleep June 19, 2018, at age 46.

Imagine a heaven of gorillas.
Imagine Koko's sudden appearance there
With her wordhoard, hundreds of teachable signs.
Imagine delighted lessons in hand-speech,

Imagine manumissions of the mute,
Joy like Beethoven's at hearing again,
As outward-spreading rings of her portable gift
Transfigure immortals into visible hymns.

Imagine manual choirs, a myriad
Innocent digits awave in unison,
Moving the nutritive empyrean air
With gales of unheard but understood song.

Imagine speechless fingers of eternity
Awaking, like Lazarus, into praise.

Gull

After Mary Oliver

Roadside lay a young black-backed gull, damaged
Near to death. Broken-winged, and mauled almost
Beyond describable ugliness, still her one
Bright remaining eye showed a fierceness to live.
We placed her gently in our bath, tubbed with towels
And the late cat's water bowl, to await
Nature's certain working. But she lived the night,
And awed us at dawn with her hunger,
Beaking eagerly each chopped cod chunk we dropped.
Soon she hobbled after us on shredded webs
And clearly craved our daily human presence.
We were overcome with hope that she would live,
But those pink feet refused to heal; they withered,
Then blackened, so that she could neither walk nor fly.
We prepared the cat's tall, carpeted castle,
Which became her daytime perch, facing seaward
Till darkness came, when we turned her round
To sit with us for nightly games with yarn,
To toss, and catch, and drop, and then repeat.
We knew that more was torn within her than
We saw, but could only feed, and watch, and wait.
How could love not be the proper word for this?

A slow decline, until one night, mid-game,
She gasped, vomited bright red blood, and died.

The Last Surviving Coastal Elephant

On the desert coast of Namibia, one
Lone elephant remains, a matriarch
With broken tusks. Orphaned, widowed and bereft,
Abandoned even by hungry poachers
Of ivory as not worth the hunt, she
Will never again feel on her face the sweet wind
Of a breathing trunk saying you are dear to me,
Or know in her bones the deep infrasound rumble
Of love from mates or offspring long since dust.

We cannot sense that lowest tone with our
Small, inadequate ears, but would feel it,
Thrumming our deepest core, if we stood
In springtime by the windy Namibian sea:
A soundless trembling in the atmosphere,
It is the offshore song of endangered great
Blue whales, all swimming south with urgency
To mate, the self-same rumble uttered once
In joy by this tusk-shattered elephant.

Now if you would rend your saddened heart,
Go there at sunset, near a certain dune
Overlooking the Atlantic. She daily comes,
To commune with the only souls in all the air
She breathes who speak a dialect of her tongue.
When cousins long sundered call, she shudders
Into song. In the air and through the ground, along
Your nerves and on your pulsing blood, you will sense
A motion, a reverberation of the mind.
You would weep to know what griefs are being shared.

Last Things

The practice has a special room for these times.
They brought her in, already calming,
And we held her warm and limp with our
Four hands, until her heart stopped. The young vet
Whispered it would only take a moment.
Then she closed her golden, trusting eyes
And went away, so quickly, so quickly,
I had no time to steel myself for the going,
But could only stroke a soft ear as it cooled.
"What else could we do, given the tumor
And her age?" I said at last to my wife,
Who moaned and rocked beside me.
"It was right to do this now," I lied.
"Later, we'll be glad we did this now," I lied.

We Made the Seas Cloacal

Killer whales, ocean's apex predator,
Cannot choose but concentrate poisonous
Humanity's sloughings. The deadliest flesh
On earth swims in orca's lovely piebald hide.

We made the seas cloacal, rivers of sludge
For them to feed in and bear their suckling young.
Sleep well tonight, my friend, knowing this:
Orca firstborn die, as mothers leach thick,
Fouled blood with ocean's strongest, darkest milk.

Now consider giving the breast to your own
Sweet, babbling first, fearing each suck will kill,
So that maybe the second can survive.
Who would bring to birth such death?
Who could nurse such grief, and live?

The Breasts of Women and of Elephants

The Maasai, tall, proud herders of cattle
In eastern Africa, warriors who will face
Hungry lions with only a spear in hand
And die fighting for their animals,
Know why the richly pouring breasts of women
And of elephants are so much alike.

Only humans and elephants, they say,
Have souls. So, like us, they will weep for love,
Will tenderly, for weeks, feed and keep alive
A dear one with a damaged trunk, and will
Deeply mourn their dead; for Maasai believe
That elephants were once our very selves.

Young brides of this tribe learn they must never
Look back when departing home, but instead
Should resolutely face their new life and
New man. Once, long ago, a fearful girl
Did turn again to her weeping mother,
And so she became the first elephant,

Her lovely breasts the nippled proofs of a
True lineage and kinship with us all.

A Tale of the Darasa of Eastern Africa

In the beginning, death was optional for all,
Even serpents and men. Then God, weary
Of the importunings of so many,
Decided that either humans or snakes must go,
And decreed a race between the two
For immortality. The first to reach Him
From the falls white men call Victoria,
Could live forever. Running along, the man
Spied a lovely woman, and stopped to woo her.
They cuddled and fondled so long the snake
Reached God first. So God said to the man when
He arrived, "Since you would rather make love
Than stay alive (I made you thus, it seems),
Only snakes may yearly renew themselves
By shedding their skins and leaving them behind."

What think you about this decision?

When My Mother Wept in Texas

When I was a child, every summer my father
Would take the Buick, my mother and me
Across country, California to the Southeast,
To visit family, hers in Alabama, his in Carolina.
He did all the driving; he loved it, and in fact
He wanted to run a long-haul truck for a living,
But Mama wouldn't let him, wanting my Dad at home.
So he loved his annual road-trip, half of it in Texas.

One year, in late summer, we drove through
The migration of tarantulas, as they crossed
Highway 80 in their thousands. We did not know then
That these all were males, marching in search of a mate.
It was, for them, a race toward death, on the way as
Roadkill or prey, or in finding a breeding female,
Who would either reject and devour the hapless,
Or else choose to mate with those you might call
The lucky, and then eat them as an afterthought,
To nourish and grow her newly-fertilized eggs.

Mama would sternly instruct my father to slow down,
And try to avoid the beautiful brown creatures;
But of course we crushed dozens, and we could not miss
The sound through the open windows in those
Un-air-conditioned days. We would hear a crunch,
And my mother would cry, weeping across Texas.

In the Midst of Life We Are in Death

Here, see this praying mantis leisurely
Masticating her late lover, who still
Jerks, headless, his glad coital dance.

Did you ever roll at highway speed through
Fat, wet clouds of swarming nectar-drugged bees?

Or drive summer asphalt across marching armies
Of migrating mate-seeking tarantulas?

Or tread upon drowned sidewalk earthworms after rain,
And the happy ants who feed upon them?

Or watch fanged spiders ushering moths into
Eternity graced with shrouds of whitest, finest silk?

In the midst of life we are in death; joyously
We breathe unthinking the common, exhaled air
Uttered in agonies of the incurable.

The Cat Who Stole My Heart

As Related by Thomas Hardy Some While after His Death

Had I lived, I would have put this story
Into verse. It tickles my heart, which rests
Today in a yew-tree box in Stinsford churchyard,
Beside my beloved Emma Gifford.
Inside the box is a cat, inside the cat
Is my heart. Inside my heart is eternal
Mirth at this, which should have been a Wessex
Tale. So I tell it now for your delight.

A grieving Nation desired my ashes
At Westminster. But my heart, I knew, belonged
To Dorset. I left appropriate instruction.
Upon its final quiver, my unthumping lump
Was severed, bloodless, wrapped in toweling and saved
In a biscuit-tin to await the mortician's
Services. Arriving, the poor man found
But an empty tin and the sated, purring
Cat of the house. Quick thinker, and fearing the loss
Of a good fee, he grabbed the offender
And wrung its furry neck. It was just the size
Of the tin and fitted nicely. Who was to know?
He bore us away to the tears of St. Michael's
Parish, and prepared us for our eternal rest.

Charlie Hannah was his name, the feline
Undertaker, and this verse shall seal his
Immortality. Come now to Dorset, friends,
Stand near my heart and purr for me and smile.

Nothing Human Is Unique

You must understand, elephants will weep:
Not only in seasonal heat of estrus
Or of musth, when lightly salted tears may
Flow unstoppably as strong sign of love,
But most of all they mourn, and massively.

We weep, of course, we grieve a dear one lost,
We know the ache, the hole torn in the side,
The emptiness unfillable with tears;
Imagine now a larger scale, a soul,
Imagine an elephantine grief.

Once, an unthinking young biologist
Played from a hidden blind the recorded voice
Of a matriarch butchered by poachers.
Wildly, for hours, her herd trumpeted
And ran about, calling in vain for their
Lost beloved. Most, at last, trooped exhausted
Away, but one lone daughter stayed, and wept
And searched with grieving cries for three long painful days.

Milton's Seeing-Eye Dog

He spoke in verses and his daughters wrote
Them down. They hated him, but I did not.
I was in fact the only one who loved
Him toward the end, he became so difficult,
An acrimonious and surly republican,
Whatever that means, I heard a servant say.
But that blind old man would scratch and rub my
Ears while he mumbled out his stories, line by line.
I took to him at once: he could not see
Me getting at the beer his Betty sent him
With his mid-day meal. She was, they said, his third
And best wife, and she brought me as a pup
To live with them and I became his dog for life.
She was more servant than bedmate, I knew,
For I slept in their room, and saw what
Rarely happened there. I had my bitches then
And knew about such things as well as any.

Here is how I earned my keep: he learned that
With my lead in his hand he could follow
Me to the jakes to squat or void, and so
The whole house was also glad I had come,
I saved them the task. I didn't mind the smell,
And I would take him back and finish his meal.
He never cared, he ate so little and drank
Even less. The beer was good, better than the food,
As my lady Betty brewed it every month.

Once a week, on the same day, the household
Left for what they called The Church. It did not
Seem to cheer them, and the blind old man refused
To go, preferring, he said, the silent Quakers,
Who were forbidden to meet. He stayed home,
Reciting his verses to me. I learned about
The Father and the Son, but never got

That Holy Ghost, who had no role, it seemed.
And that first man, who loved his wife more than God—
A good thing, too, she was more loveable.
That petulant Father seemed a cur, but
Satan I liked the best, so brave and adamant:
Truth to tell, he made me think of me.
And I would have liked to know that Eve, she
Reminded me of my mistress, Betty,
Docile, and giving, but steely within.

But for poor eyeless Samson I felt most sad:
I wondered how he ever found the jakes.

Dog

This Man worships Me.
I am his Dog.
Daily he offers Me delicious Food
And saves my Shit in little Plastic Bags.
He takes me out by Night to Grace
The Neighbors' Grass and Trees
And leave my Manly Mark
For every passing Lovelorn Bitch.
He restores my Water Bowl.
Life is Good.

When my Brother died by Enemy Car
This Man howled and ran About
As if there were no Heaven of Dogs,
Where Rabbits will run before us Forever
And Squirrels sport on the Green,
Where every Tree will shout of Me
And lovely Bitches Flock
To my enticing Musk.
Death is Good for Dogs as Well.

Uh-Oh! Dinner!

The Wolf of Gubbio

*During renovations in Gubbio of the Church of St. Francis of Peace,
in the year 1872, the skeleton of a large wolf, apparently several centuries old,
was found under a slab near the church wall.*
—Adrian House, *Francis of Assisi*

I have no name your kind would know;
We go by scent, my name's a smell,
But who I am one word will tell:
I ate the sheep of Gubbio.

Soon I grew bold, first lambs, then men,
For you were fat, and I was thin.
To kill, to eat, my only good:
I chewed your tongues, I lapped your blood.

I knew no God, I murdered sheep:
Fill my belly, go to sleep.
Your children next, such easy prey
When they came daily out to play.

Then "Brother Wolf," he said to me,
And all was changed, changed utterly.
I wept ashamed, he stroked my head
And promised me I would be fed.

Now I'm a lamb, and I am meek,
They feed me richly every week.
I live by what dear Francis said:
It's meat and blood, but tastes like bread.

A Shepherd, Twenty-Four December

After Tom Hennen

Sheep huddle, penned, crowding against the dark
And breath-fogging chill. Some few doze. Most listen,
Large-eyed. They have heard the wolves. Armed with dogs,
I watch, knowing what burdens these creatures
Must bear: teeth of predators, knives of butchers,
A reputation for stupidity, their comical
Look after giving up, so patiently, their fleece.
But tonight was born the tiny Lamb of God.

Now, forever aureoled in metaphor,
Sheep may safely graze unafraid, overseen
By these brave figures of speech, Good Shepherds,
We like to say, ennobled alike with our flocks.

Whatever snows may come, whatever wolves,
This night we herders say *Gloria in Excelsis Deo.*

When Elephants Dance

In Thailand, aged, blinded elephants dance
To the piano of volunteer Paul Barton,
Whose musical love for animals will
Alter your saddened heart. At a sanctuary
For abused and damaged working elephants
He has placed a vintage upright in a meadow.
When he plays her favorite Beethoven, Lam Duan
("Yellow-Flowered Tree"), her crusted eyes streaming,
Will slowly pace from the bush, trunk tip testing
Each unsighted step before her like a white cane.
Then, standing by the unseen instrument, entranced
By the sonata called *Pathetique,* she will sway
To its rhythms, raised to a purity of love
Our own poor clouded hearts may never know.

Her friend Romsai, partially blind, prefers Bach.
The architectural simplicities
Of the Twenty-Fifth Goldberg raise him to
A rhythmical trance every god would envy.
While Barton plays, a rapt Romsai sways
In a sarabande of elephantine joy.

Whose heart would not yearn for an elephant
Soul in the face of such divine delight?

Dominus Illuminatio Mea

Behold, the simplest eye imaginable,
A single cell, an eater of the light—
The photosynthesizing bacterium
Synechocystis, one small, determined

Seeker after enlightenment, will swim,
Olympian, toward any brightness through
The dark, lashing with love its flagella,
Filled with yearning for the stars,

Its jellied wall a lens, focusing
Photons to feed, and to approach its only god,
The sun. Here, in phototaxis, life's longing
For the light, lies the origin of eyes,

The first of all visionary seers:
Dominus illuminatio mea.

Life Builds Eyes at Need

Life builds eyes at need, a jelly to let
The light come in, and makes them fade, as well:
Pale blind cavefish feel, not see; with endless
Night, eyes fall vestige, costly luxury.

Before sight, no scene yearned for seers,
No sky blued for us. Fear forced eyes upon flesh:
We are mice, and the dark fills with owls;
Spawn, floating in a wash of famished jaws.

Maybe no vision in eternity either,
No loveliness without the lens to view it;
What if retrospect were the only heaven,
Just the memory of love and wonder?

Open your eyes, see what you can with them,
Now, before they both fold shut forever.

At a Wake of Elephants

In Botswana once, I found a ruined hulk,
Her grey hide streaked with vultures' dung, both tusks
Intact. Not poachers, then, but nature's work.
Then I saw the scorches down her stiffened leg,
Sign a lightning-bolt had claimed this matriarch
As she fed upon the greenness in her prime.
Moved, I promised myself I would return, as to
A Sunday churchyard, all that year, to watch
Her yielding back, ungrudged, her every precious gift.

How soon God cleans and purifies all whitest bones!
Two seasons' work and it was done: nesting birds
Had claimed the hairs, jackals and scavengers
The hide, after vultures, lions, and smaller fry
Stripped the softer flesh. But there remained a wake
To perform, some memorial to all this love
And joy, now gone back to the source. I knew
Her migrant herd would return with the rain, and so
Would I, to watch and, I hoped, to grieve with them.

The season came round again, and crowds to graze.
I saw a group approach the gleaming skull,
As to a holy place. All vocalizing ceased.
Like loved ones silent at an open grave, they stood,
Until their matriarch first nosed a tusk,
Most tenderly, from base to point. Then she grasped
It with her nostrils' tip, and tugged, and rocked
And wrapped it around with massive love while rumbling
Deepest words of grief I could not grasp, but feel still
Within my heart's core. Then each adult performed
The same slow, sacred rite, while their young ones
Gamboled, as in a shining field of tombs.

A long hour passed, and still, they reminisced
And mourned. The hot sun set, and still, they mourned.
Then most, at last, trooped thirsting away, save one tall
Female, daughter, I guessed, to those beloved bones;
She remained, silent, to touch each scattered part.

There Will Come Soft Rains

After Sara Teasdale

There will come soft rains and the smell of earth,
And tree frogs creaking unlimited joys.

The mockingbird's throat will swell for love
Through long days emptied of human noise.

Swallows will build their houses of mud
Moistened, enriched, with human blood.

Not one will know our war is done,
Not one will care that no side won.

Not one will grieve, neither bird nor tree,
That mankind perished utterly.

And Earth, refreshed when she wakes at dawn,
Will cleanse herself now we are gone.

How Chukwu's Message Went Awry

Let me tell you a tale of the Igbo,
How Chukwu, whom some call Allah or Dieu,
Sent a dog to earth with the best of news
For those who fear and those who grieve alone:
Smear your dead with ash and bury them lovingly,
And they will come again to live with you.

But the dog grew weary on that long trek,
And rested beside a river of stars.
He lingered, loving the shining flow.

So Chukwu sent a second messenger,
A sheep, more dependable, less intelligent,
Who remembered but half the secret:
Bury your dead. He was from Chukwu,
And that is what we do, from of old.

So death was not meant to be permanent,
And we no longer listen to sheep.

Recycle

Just think of it: one day the bits of you
Will grace again the biosphere, and,
In due course, the universe, to nourish
And rejoice a tree, a tiger, your descendants,

Another star. Best to burn cleanly to
Soft powder and ash; soon, soon, you may be
Life again, and your bones marble for
Tomorrow's shining Michelangelo.

Scatter, fly as wind, fall as rain upon
All you love. Let them drink you in their wine,
And revel, and bear strong young to be flesh
Of your flesh. Or, perhaps, what better fate

Than to soar part of the eye of a hawk,
Or the vast, breaching fluke of a great blue whale?

How the Fabled Toktokkie Beetle Prays for a Drink

Nightly the chill Namibian sea
Sends a welcome onshore breeze
And with it a thick, wet fog,
Heaven's only gift of moisture
To the desert Skeleton Coast.
And here the well-named toktokkie beetle
Kneels with its face to the earth.

After an evening of love, clicking
Their tok-tok call to attract any willing mates,
They will climb to the crest of a dune,
Face west, tip their heads to the ground,
Legs straight up, and pray to the god
Of water. Tiny fog-droplets
Gather on limbs and carapace,
Awaiting sufficient mass
For gravity to pull them down
Toward a thousand thirsting mouths.
They drink until full, half-doubling
Their body weight, then burrow
Into the sand for a cooling
And contented day of rest.
Not a bad life, this.

A Prayer to Converse with Animals

In Honor of Greta Thunberg

Grant me, please, the ear of the bat,
To hear each whisper in the air,
And the innocent tongue of the ox,
To mouth the sweet grass only.
Let me cross over and inhabit
The mockingbird's throat, to sing
Aloud of my shame. Help me
Abandon murderous humanity,
That I may apologize, and be
Understood, and say how sorry
I am for all we have done to them,
And will do, before our time is up:
For the knife at the throat of the lamb,
For the tiger's cage, the crushed
Testicles of the baited bull,
The pink-nosed lab rat dismembered alive,
And the overheated earth our legacy.
Let me beg them to hold on,
Stay alive until humankind
Is finished, and imagine how graced
Their world could be
When we are gone.

About the Author

Until his retirement in 2007, Randel McCraw Helms was a professor of English at Arizona State University, where he taught classes in the Romantic poets, Shakespeare, and the Bible as literature. His published books include *Tolkien's World, Who Wrote the Gospels?* and *Gospel Fictions.* Making poems has been his lifelong obsessive avocation. He lives near Phoenix with his wife and cats.

www.ingramcontent.com/pod-product-compliance
Lightning Source LLC
Chambersburg PA
CBHW071642090426
42738CB00013B/3186